SUMMER

in the Forest

A *Seasons in the Forest* book

Field Guides for Little Naturalists

First Edition
ISBN 979-8-9864703-6-8

For Monique and Helen,
who took their children into nature.

High in the forest on a
hot summer day

a young eagle looks out

and then soars away.

Squirrels jump
from branches in
rambunctious play

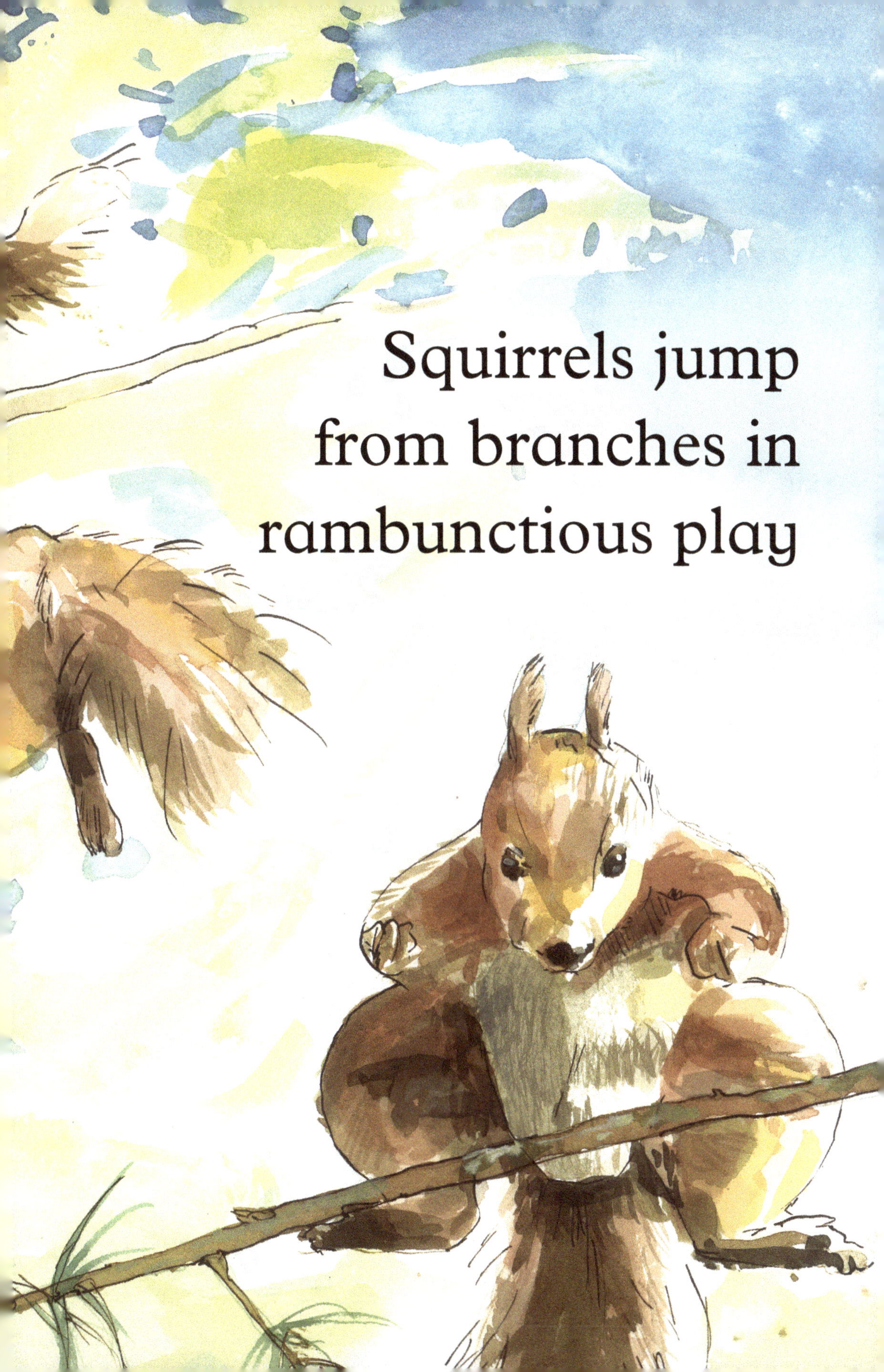

high in the forest
on a hot summer day.

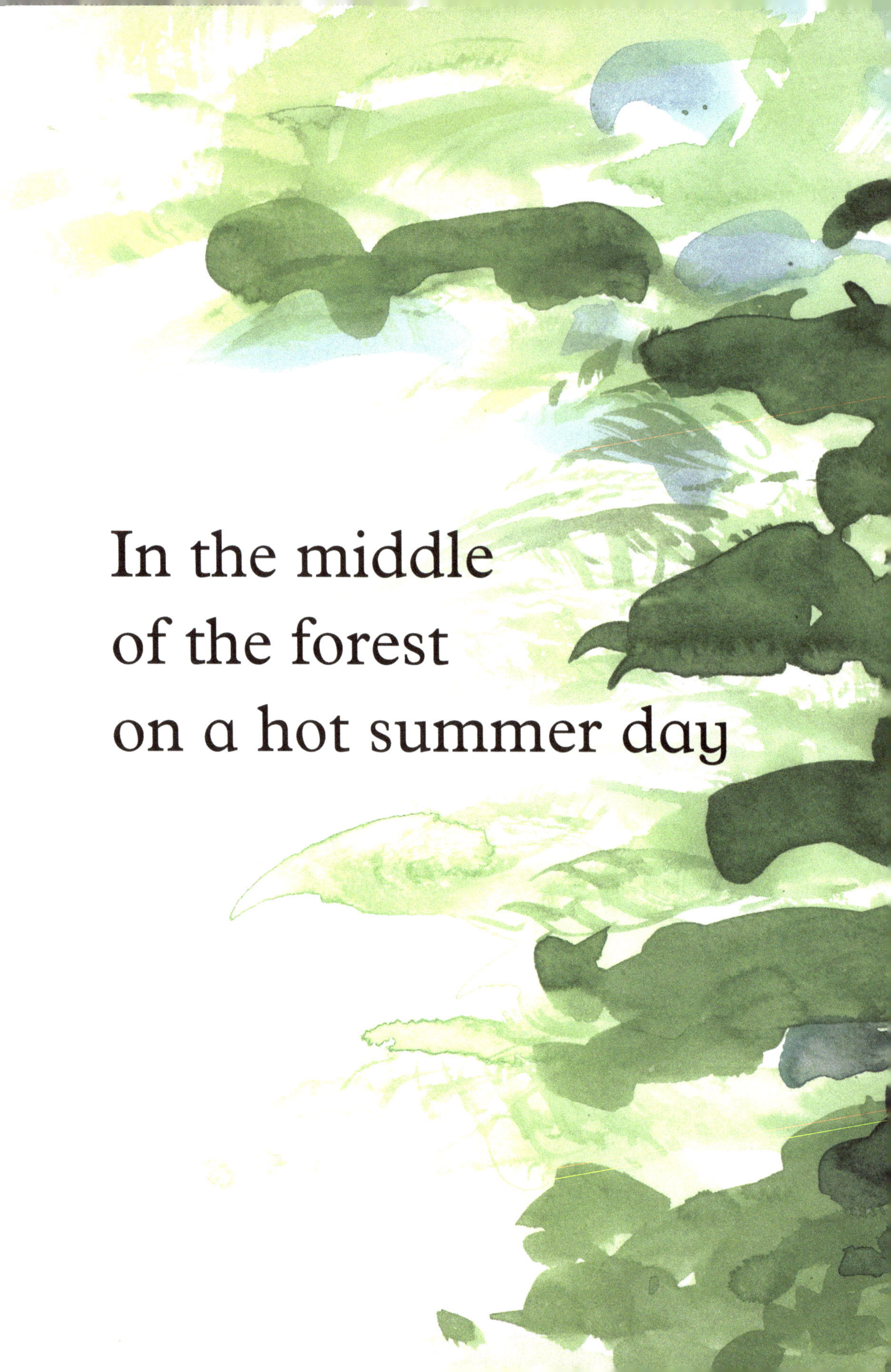

In the middle
of the forest
on a hot summer day

chips from a
Pileated fly
every which way.

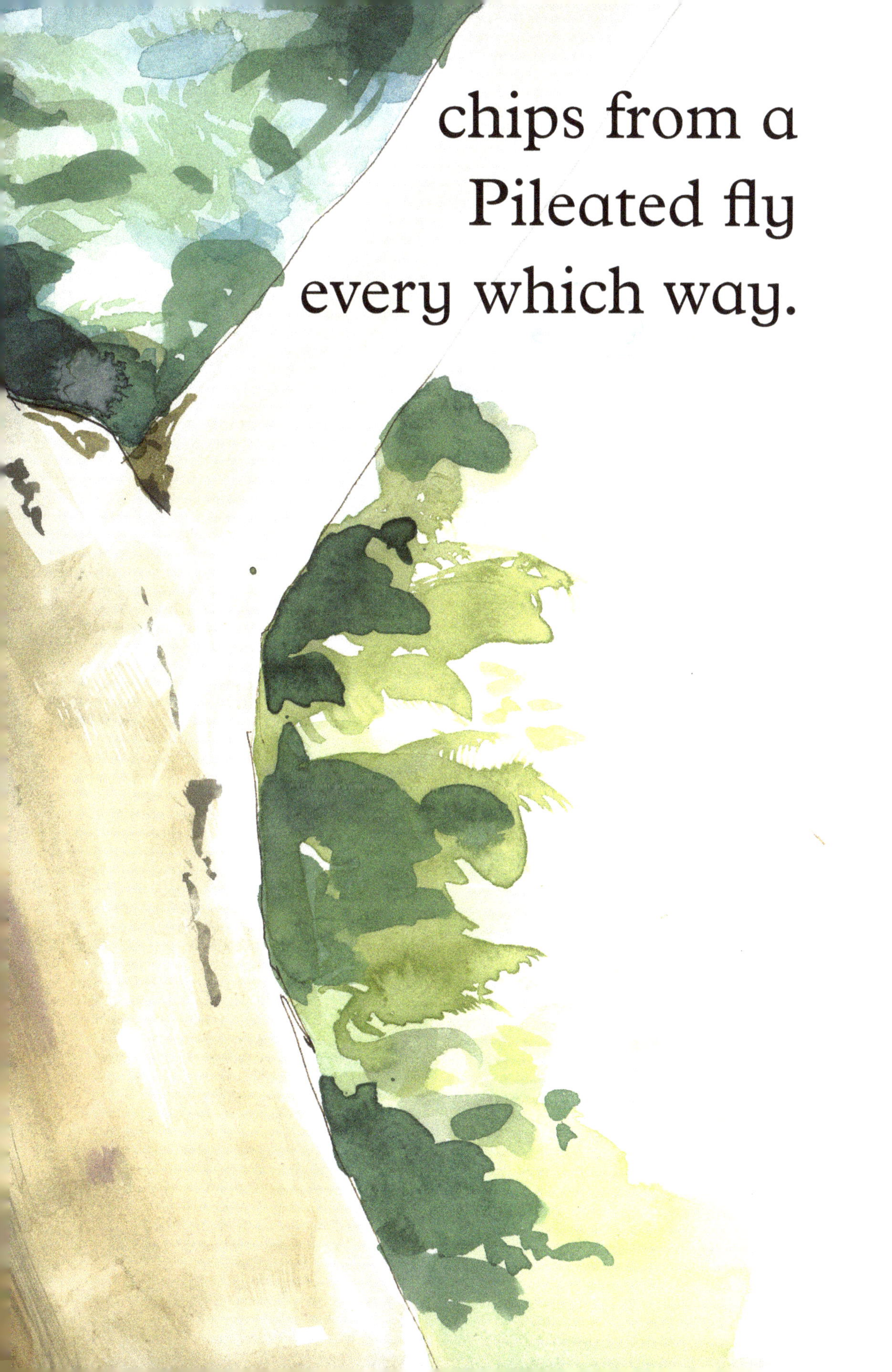

Ma racoon must decide
if to come or to stay

in the middle
of the forest
on a hot summer day.

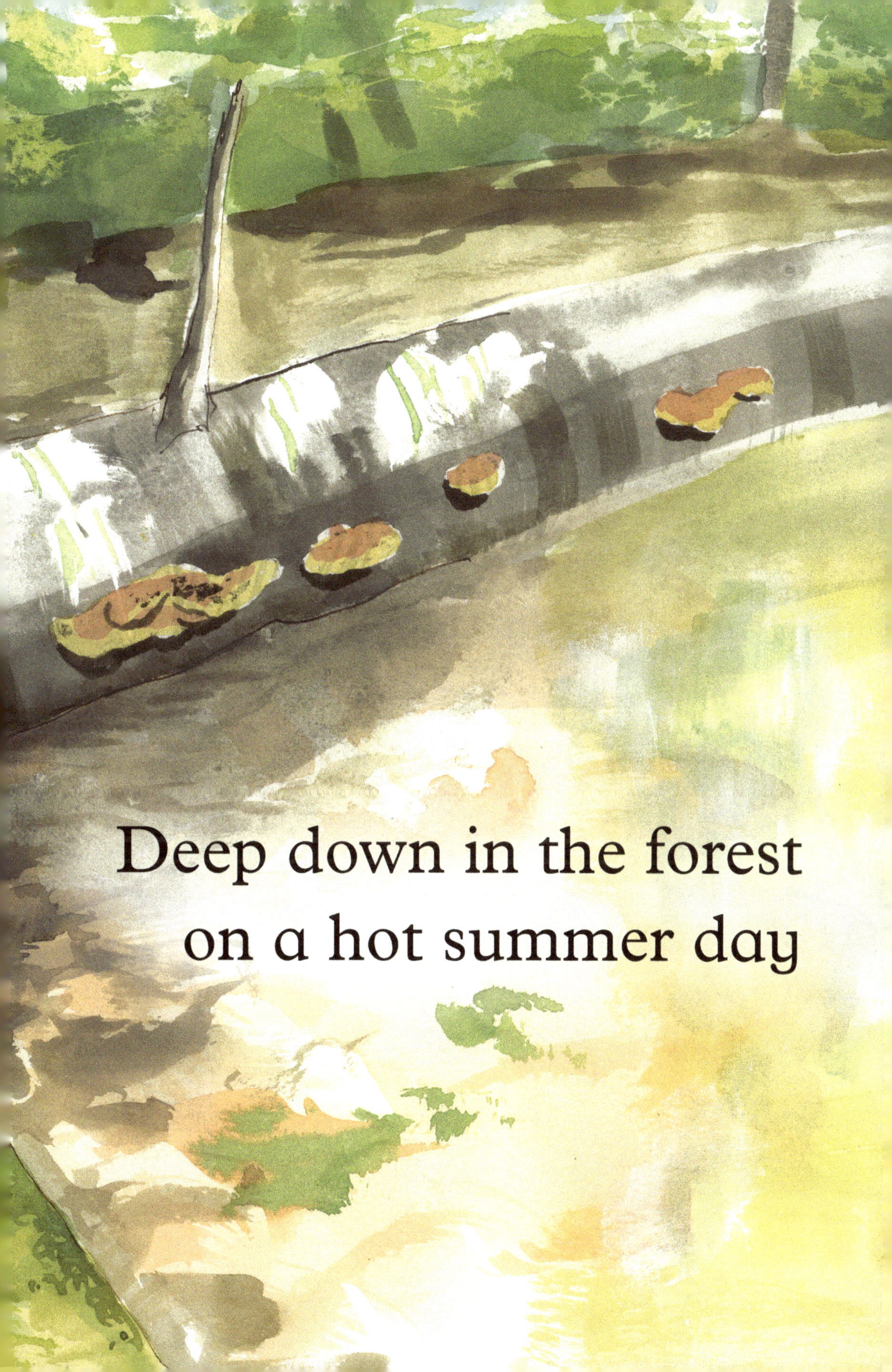

Deep down in the forest
on a hot summer day

the soft ground is cool,
the shadows are grey.

Icy cold water
gurgles up from the clay

deep down in the forest

on a hot summer day.

People in the city live in tall buildings that have different levels. An elevator or stairs take them up. These levels are called floors or stories - first story, second story, and so on. The forest also has stories. The highest is called the overstory, the middle is called the understory and then there is the ground floor or the forest floor.

The next time you go up stairs, can you pretend you are a little animal scampering up to the overstory?

About the author:

Christine Copeland lives in the forest of Massachusetts with her husband Bill, a pediatrician, naturalist and teacher, and their dogs and cat. Her sons have fledged but return seasonally. She is grateful to be visited by many birds and other animals throughout the year. Christine has a BFA from Cornell University and a Masters in Education from Antioch New England. She is an author/illustrator and also paints in oil. Her work can be seen at christinecopelandbooks.com and bcc-studios.com/paintings.

www.ingramcontent.com/pod-product-compliance
Lightning Source LLC
Chambersburg PA
CBHW042334030426
42335CB00027B/3342